The Testimony of a Disciple

Meet My Friend, Reverend Fred

By Jeff Johnson

WORD & SPIRIT
PUBLISHING

The Testimony of a Disciple
Meet My Friend, Reverend Fred
ISBN: 978-1-949106-35-0

Published by Word and Spirit Publishing
P.O. Box 701403
Tulsa, Oklahoma 74170
wordandspiritpublishing.com

Dedication

To my mentor and good friend, Reverend Fred Young. Some of God's greatest gifts come in peculiar packages.

A special thank you to our friend Carrie Ludescher for allowing us to use her beautiful painting as the cover art for this book. Your faith and your fight continue to inspire us all as we look to His cross.

Table of Contents

Introduction

Not too long ago, a friend of mine told me that he thought my relationship with Reverend Fred Young was both unusual and wonderful. When he asked me to recall how a seventy-year-old, African American prison minister and itinerant evangelist would come to be such a good friend and mentor to a middle-aged white man living in a country club, it really caught me off guard. That's when it occurred to me that I hadn't really given much thought to my twelve-year walk with this man—a man that I so admired and respected; a man who has so blessed and changed my life forever. So, I set out to tell him the story of how we met—a story that truly shows how God can change our lives through the most unexpected people, often in very unlikely places, and under some unusual circumstances.

In February of 2002, I found myself at the end of myself. After thirty-four years of living a life trying to chase down everything that this world had to offer, I realized that I could never fill the emptiness that I felt within, and that emptiness soon turned to a gripping fear that I could not seem to shake. As my wife, Kathleen, then two months pregnant with our daughter, Kendall, lay next to me sleeping, I tossed and turned all night in great torment. My selfish mind could only find relief in thinking of how I could and would end my life. I could see no other way out for me, I was truly lost in darkness with nowhere to turn.

At the pinnacle moment of my despair, I grasped for what I today call my final lifeline, and spoke these words in my heart, *Jesus, if you are real, please be real to me right now.* And that's when the Lord spoke to me, not with an audible voice, but into my heart with the two shortest words I had ever heard. He simply said "I Am." When He spoke these words, I felt the Holy

Spirit of God rush into every fiber of my being. In an instant I knew that I had gone from death to life. I immediately began to weep, and the tears began to flow in a way that is still beyond my understanding today. It was as if the streams of living water that Jesus talks about literally rose up in me and came gushing out of my eyes, completely soaking my pillow. What I didn't know at that moment, but do know today, is that I didn't have to die that day because Jesus had already died for me, and when He rose again, I was raised with Him. In that one moment, I was set free forever from the tyranny of sin.

For the next three years, as I tried to comprehend and describe what had happened to me that February morning at 5:55 a.m., the words always seemed to fail me, and they fail me even today. All that I can say for sure is that Jesus is real, He's risen, and He's ready to receive anyone who would call on His name (see Romans 10:13). His grace and mercy still overwhelm me today when I recall how my greatest encounter and experience with Him happened to me at the very moment that I deserved it the least. He literally took my sentence of death and gave me eternal life instead. Today my life stands as a testimony to the goodness and mercy of God, and I long to tell the world that what He did for me, He will do for anyone who simply looks to Him.

When you are a babe in Christ, you are much like a newborn baby in so many ways. Although your spirit has been completely sealed, restored, and renewed by the Holy Spirit, it takes time to learn and grow in your knowledge and experience of what you actually possess. In other words, even though your spirit has been perfected, your flesh (unrenewed mind and corrupted body) doesn't exactly want to cooperate with the leadings and promptings of your new spirit. This takes time, patience, and a whole boatload of God's grace and mercy as you learn to grow and walk in this new spiritual state. And just like a real baby, you need to have mature believers in Christ feed you, care for you, and teach you how to walk and talk. And this brings me to the story of how I met Reverend Fred.

When my family and I joined Beach Church in Jacksonville Beach, Florida, we did it for the simple reason that our daughter was already attending their preschool and we really liked the people we were meeting. As new members we were given a questionnaire asking which of their many ministries we might be interested in serving under, and after reviewing the entire list I could not find any that caught my eye. Having recently watched a segment on TBN about Prison Fellowship, the prison ministry started by Chuck Colson, I filled in the last line on the form entitled "Other" with the words *Prison Ministry* and quickly turned in my form.

About a week after turning in my volunteer form, I received a phone call from Carmen Johns, a pastor at the church, who also just happened to be blind. I almost laughed when she said to me "I ***see*** that you have an interest in Prison Ministry." At that point I really felt like the Lord was messing with me and I could do nothing but laugh. I somewhat reluctantly gave her permission to give my name and number to a gentleman named Doug Berle. Doug was the volunteer coordinator for the church's prison ministry outreach, and he also just happened to be the nephew of comedic legend Milton Berle. From there the story gets even more humorous. After meeting with Doug at a local restaurant, I found myself suddenly being whisked into prison ministry, and after some paperwork and a background check, I was approved and ready to go on my first visit to Florida State Prison.

After meeting up with Doug and another gentleman named Ed Washburn on a cool Saturday morning, I found myself somewhat nervous as I rode in the back of Doug's giant crimson Cadillac towards one of the worst places on earth. To add to my already anxious state, Doug and Ed began to mess with me by telling me about a gentleman named Reverend Fred that we were planning to pick up along the way. Ed jokingly asked Doug, "Do you think we should put Fred in the front seat, or have him ride in the back with Jeff?" and then they both burst into laughter. As if I wasn't nervous enough, now they wanted to make me take this hour-and-a-half long drive with someone who may or may not have a screw loose. I had no idea what I was in for.

There are moments in your life when you know that you have been set up by God, moments when you know He has placed a divine appointment on your calendar, an appointment that you would have no way at all to prepare for. From the moment that I met Reverend Fred, I felt like I had known him my entire life. I can't recall what we spoke about riding out to the prison that day, or what we talked about the rest of that day, but what I did know for sure was that the Lord had placed someone that was very dear to His heart in my path. Sometimes all that we can recall in a special moment is that God is with us, and in those moments, we are reminded that His presence is all we need. We are also humorously reminded that He chooses to place His Spirit in some very unusual and unexpected containers (see 2 Corinthians 4:7).

Not long after meeting Reverend Fred, we began spending a lot of time together over breakfasts, lunches, and most importantly—serving together through his ministry. I not only loved the man because I loved Christ who I was seeing in Him, but I also loved the way he did ministry work. I guess the best way to describe Reverend Fred is that he is a mobile church with arms and legs. His life and ministry is all about taking the church of Christ to people each and every day through both planned events, and all of the unplanned events that God orchestrates along the way. I have been amazed and overwhelmed by how many times I have seen God work through and around Reverend Fred when we were simply on our way to somewhere else. We could have plans to visit Florida State Prison, but it was often what happened on our way out to the prison that astonished me the most.

Reverend Fred has always taught me that we are all ministers of God, and that there is such joy in living a lifestyle of ministry 24/7/365. He has taught me that this life in Christ is not so much about what we do, but who we are in Him.

My purpose in writing this book is to honor God by honoring the gift that He has given me in my great mentor, friend, and spiritual helper. I want to share with you some of my favorite inspirational life lessons and stories that the Lord has blessed me with over the years through the words and actions of this humble man of God. I have titled each of these lessons with some of the many catch phrases that Reverend Fred is famously known for in our circles of influence. When I have shared these stories with others over the years, I have always been delighted at how much insight, joy, and laughter they bring. Invariably, with every little story or teaching that I share, I am often struck by the comment that follows, "I would really love to meet this

Reverend Fred." Well, my friend, today is your day to meet the man they call Reverend Fred.

Weeping May Last for a Night

One of the first lessons that I learned as a babe in Christ was that the euphoric feeling that we often experience after receiving Christ is soon followed by a period of great trial or testing. I am reminded that Jesus, after being baptized in the Holy Spirit, was led by the same Spirit into the wilderness, where He was tempted by Satan for forty days and forty nights. When Jesus was tempted, He was tempted on our behalf, so that today He can relate to us when we (of our own free will) are led astray by the lusts and lure of this fallen world.

My first period of trial and testing happened shortly after I met Reverend Fred. My first few years as a new believer could best be described as being in love, in a state of great euphoria. My experience of this joy soon began to fade, and I found myself engaged in a great battle within. I was gripped with a heavy cloud of fear that seemed like it would never lift. While staring into the open refrigerator one morning for way too long, I began to cry, which immediately drew the attention of my wife in the other room. When she asked me what was wrong with me (a question she asks quite often), I tried to explain to her how this great cloud of fear was gripping my heart. Without hesitation she said, "Why don't you call Reverend Fred?" Immediately I felt as if she had given me a much-needed answer.

After marching upstairs to my office, I quickly, although somewhat reluctantly, called my new friend. Through the speaker phone on my desk I began to describe to him, in the best detail I could, the great fear and dread that was pummeling me. After a long pause, with my forehead now resting on my desk, I suddenly heard the most beautiful voice begin to sing. At first, I was taken aback, because I clearly had not requested a tune, but to my delight I found myself calmed by the song that Rev was singing. *"Jesus loves me this I know, for the Bible tells me so, little ones to Him belong, we are weak, but He is strong."* Immediately I began to weep, and as I did, I could feel that spirit of heaviness lifting off of me, only to be replaced by the Spirit of God which had welled up in my spirit, once again setting me free.

After agreeing to meet Reverend Fred for lunch later that same day, we began to discuss what I had experienced earlier that morning, and I couldn't help but thank God for giving me a friend to call. A friend who not only knew exactly what I was going through, but who had been there himself a time or two, and could help me walk through it. As we reminisced about the goodness of the Lord, he looked over at me from the passenger seat of my car and said, "Jeff, weeping may last for a night, but joy always comes in the morning." When he spoke those words over me it hit me like a lightning bolt, and I knew in my spirit that what he had spoken over me was the Word of God. The reason that the Word had such power was because it was mixed with his faith in that Word, a faith that came by his experiences with the Lord. That moment still reminds me today that the Word of God (Jesus) is not only to be understood with our logic, but He is to be experienced in real and tangible ways through our spirits. Truly, we have a friend that sticks closer than a brother.

Scripture References:

"For His anger lasts only a moment, but His favor lasts a lifetime: weeping may come at night, but rejoicing comes in the morning." (Psalm 30:5 NIV)

"And whenever the tormenting spirit from God troubled Saul, David would play the harp. Then Saul would feel better, and the tormenting spirit would go away." (1 Samuel 16:23)

"For God hath not given us the spirit of fear; but of power, and of love, and of a sound mind." (2 Timothy 1:7 KJV)

No Skip Courses

No one ever walks through life undefeated. We live in a fallen world and are surrounded by death in its numerous forms and fashions. We all experience loss, grief, depression, sickness, and poverty in varying forms. And whether our issues are caused by our own bad decisions, or by the bad decisions of others, we cannot escape from the fallen nature of humanity and its ongoing effects on this world. Although God is not the author of the sin we find in today's world, He is the author and finisher of our faith in Christ, who took away all sin when He nailed our old sin nature to His cross. Our old man was nailed to the cross, and when Jesus was raised up by the Holy Spirit, we too were raised up to new life by the matrimony of His Spirit and ours.

What I am starting to see and experience today in my union with Christ, seemed absent when I was just a babe in Christ. I thank God for my mentor Reverend Fred who always taught me that pain was part of the process in this walk of Faith. I could have made suffering avoidance into an art form by the way I tried to constantly maneuver around the aches and pains of life. But Reverend Fred always told me that there were no "skip courses" and that I would have to walk the way of the cross.

Sure, I had experienced God's glory when Christ sealed my spirit with His, and this glory has been promised and given freely by the Lord, but He also promised that it would always be preceded by the sufferings of this present world. I am so grateful to have a mentor who could tell me that I would be OK, and that what I was going through, he had gone through also, and that just as he walked through the valley, I too would walk through the valley. Reverend Fred always assured me that the Lord was walking right alongside me, even in my darkest most fretful moments in life. And I always made it to the other side just like he said I would.

You might as well face it, in this world you will have trouble, but Jesus encourages you to cheer up, because He has overcome the world, and through your spiritual union with Him, you too will overcome. The moment that you discover that your suffering today is always followed by His glory tomorrow, hope rises and you will find yourself resting safely under His shelter. When you hear His still small voice telling you to rise, you can rise in His power and can walk confidently through any fire and over any flood. God never promised that life would be without storm or tempest, but He has assured you that you will make it to the other side. So, rest assured, your sins are forgiven. Let that thought alone bring you the joy and assurance you need today, as you walk through the wind, the fire, and the flood. You will surely come out on the other side where you will find the Son shining in your heart.

Scripture References:

"For I reckon that the sufferings of this present time are not worthy to be compared with the glory which shall be revealed in us." (Romans 8:18 KJV)

"I have told you all this so that you may have peace in me. Here on earth you will have many trials and sorrows. But take heart, because I have overcome the world." (John 16:33)

"When you go through deep waters I will be with you. When you go through rivers of difficulty, you will not drown. When you walk through the fire of oppression, you will not be burned up; the flames will not consume you." (Isaiah 43:2)

Believe in Your Own Prayers

When I first met Reverend Fred, I was like a baby plant, whose root system in God's Word did not run very deep. Although I was pushing off a few leaves and some tiny fruit, a good storm could have blown me away. For this reason, I really exhausted my friends who were more mature in their faith, and none more so than Rev.

I called him constantly for prayer, most often when I was being attacked by the enemy with great and fearful torment. I remember one time calling him early in the morning while traveling to New Jersey. I had a huge meeting with the chairman of our company who was in town from India and I had gone out drinking the night before with two coworkers, a decision that put me in a prison of my own making. I was awakened at 4:00 a.m. with a terrible feeling of condemnation from the enemy for having committed such a stupid act, and felt like I was destined to completely destroy my career, as I was in no condition to give my presentation scheduled for later that morning.

In my panic I called Reverend Fred, and upon getting his voicemail I left him a very distressed message. After showering and getting myself ready, I was still in great turmoil, extremely hung over and feeling worse by the moment. As I entered our corporate office, I quickly rushed to the bathroom to wash my face and try to straighten myself out. As I was leaving the restroom, I noticed that I had received a voicemail from my friend.

As I stood outside the bathroom in the hallway of our offices I listened to his message. As I listened it became clear that this was no ordinary message; it was actually a prayer for me that he was making to God. I can't recall much of what the message said, but I remember it being a heart-felt petition to our Father to "calm me down" and to assure me that I was forgiven. As I listened to that message, the peace of God, like I had rarely felt, rushed over every fiber of my being and I felt the life and health of the Holy Spirit rush through my body. I was not only reenergized but actually felt very calm and confident as I became aware that God's Spirit had rested on me through this prayer made in faith in the goodness and mercy of a loving Father. My hangover was completely gone and my presentation that I gave that morning was one of my best ever!

Since that day, Rev has encouraged me on numerous occasions to "develop my own prayer life." He told me one day (and this made me laugh) that God was going to move me from the back of the prayer line to the front, where I could pray for others. He assured me that one day God would give me faith to believe in my own prayers as much as I did the prayers of others. God, through Reverend Fred, has taught me well (and is still teaching me today) that when Jesus died for us, He not only took our sin nature, but He gave us His righteous nature. And the Bible says that the prayers of a righteous man are powerful and effective. Today, thanks be to God, I believe in my own prayers, not because I am good, but because the one who died to make me right with Him is good. And when He gave me His Spirit, He gave me His access to a powerful prayer life.

Scripture References:

"But grow in grace, and in the knowledge of our Lord and Savior Jesus Christ. To Him be glory both now and forever. Amen." (2 Peter 3:18 KJV)

"I am praying not only for these disciples but also for ALL who will ever believe in me through their message. I pray that they will ALL be one, just as you and I are one—as you are in me, Father, and I am in you. And may they be in us so that the world will believe you sent me." (John 17:20-21)

"God made Him who knew no sin to be sin for us, so that IN HIM we might become the righteousness of God." (2 Corinthians 5:21 NIV)

"Therefore confess your sins to each other and pray for each other so that you may be healed. The prayer of a righteous person is powerful and effective." (James 5:16 NIV)

Coming Out from the Kitchen

Over the past twelve years I have had countless lunches with Reverend Fred. These somewhat ordinary lunches have often taken an extraordinary (extra-ordinary) turn by some divine visit paid to our table. Invariably, the visitor will say something to the effect of "Hey, I know you. You came to visit me when I was in county jail several years ago." Or, "Hey, do you visit people in XYZ prison?" Most have been men, but there was one occasion when the female manager of a BBQ restaurant walked right up to our table and thanked Rev for a visit he had paid to her when she was at a youth detention center seven years prior. One by one, these souls, precious to God, have come out from the kitchen to pay a surprise visit to the humble man who had paid them a visit during one of the lowest points in their life.

These occurrences had become so frequent that at one point I jokingly asked Reverend Fred if he was staging them. His simple, humble reply was, "I think the Lord has set these up for your benefit, Jeff." And I think he was 100 percent right! I think God wanted to show me how one man, who obediently went and visited people in distress, day in and day out for nearly forty years, was now seeing a fruitful harvest from all the seeds he had sown. How one man, through simple obedience, can show Jesus to those in need.

One gentleman who approached us was a district manager for a Zaxby's Restaurant where we "just happened" to be eating. He recalled getting a visit from Reverend Fred in the county jail more than a decade prior, after he had been arrested for murder. He had murdered the man who had been molesting his three-year-old niece, and was given a twenty-year sentence for his crime. Through the grace and mercy of God, he was released after serving only seven years, and upon his release, he found only one place that would give him a job. You guessed it, Zaxby's! He had worked his way up from cleaning the bathrooms and tables, all the way up through the ranks of the company to district manager, overseeing twelve area restaurants. And we just "happened" to be there at that one restaurant on that one day, to receive a reciprocal visit from a man who had been visited on one of the worst days of his life. You can call it random, but I call it God's rhythm.

If you think that living a simple, quiet life with God is boring and un-impactful, then you haven't met Reverend Fred or any of the people whose lives he has touched. If you think that you cannot change this world by one simple act of kindness at a time, then you are dead wrong. We change this world when we purposefully walk with God, and allow His Spirit to change just one life at a time, one encounter at a time. I want you to see that regardless of what you do for a living, God can give you His real life. He can give you a life that has such meaning and purpose, and He will build His life in you one encounter at a time, as you reach out to one person a time.

From this point forward, focus your attention on God's never-ending presence in your life. Go out today with this purpose—to change just one life, one moment at a time. Let every appointment you have today become a divine appointment, and watch His power flow through you and change your surroundings. May His Kingdom come today in you!

Scripture References:

"Whatever you do [no matter what it is] in word or deed, do everything in the name of The Lord Jesus [and in dependence on Him], giving thanks to God the Father through Him." (Colossians 3:17 AMP)

"For I was hungry and you fed me; I was thirsty and you gave me water; I was a stranger and you invited me into your homes; naked and you clothed

me; sick and in prison, and you visited me." (Matthew 25:35-36 TLB)

"Verily, verily, I say to you, he that believeth on me, the works that I do shall he do also; and greater works than these shall he do; because I go to my Father. And whatsoever ye shall ask in my name, that I will do, that the Father may be glorified in the Son. If ye shall ask anything in my name, I will do it. If you love me, keep my commandments. And I will pray the Father, and he shall give you another Comforter, that he may abide with you forever; even the Spirit of truth; whom the world cannot receive, because it seeth him not, neither knoweth him: but ye know him; for he dwelleth with you and shall be in you." (John 14:12-17 KJV)

Look for the Greater Qualities

There are very few people in this world who will try to encourage everyone they meet. People who, from the moment that they meet you, look for your best qualities instead of your worst. Reverend Fred is certainly one of those people. As I write this, I am having trouble recalling one time where he has ever spoken negatively about someone behind their back. Don't get me wrong, he has corrected me a time or two, but even in his correction he can always make me laugh about my foibles, and his love for me makes me want to come up higher. When someone makes you see that you have Christ in you through the Holy Spirit, you are inspired to live this holy consecrated life that God has planned for you. I think that is why Jesus instructed us to be perfect, just like our Father in Heaven (see Matthew 5:48).

This world today loves to point the finger of blame at everyone, but seldom does anyone look within themselves for God-guided introspection. If we had a T-shirt that could aptly describe today's society, I believe it would read "It's not my fault." God calls us to change this world, that is certain, but He calls us to do it from the inside out. Truly, the only person that you can change is yourself, and real change takes place in your spirit through the direction and operation of the Holy Spirit in you. But I can assure you that once you desire change, you only need to take the first step, and that's when the Holy Spirit comes along side you to lead and guide you.

Reverend Fred has taught me well over the years to "look for the greater qualities in people." He has taught me that it's both easy and lazy to sit back in a puffed-up state of mind and pick other people apart. But a real man or woman of God will always dig deep to find the good in each and every person because God is good, and we are created in His image. Sure, sometimes we have to get through a pound of flesh to get to one ounce of spirit, but when we dig deep, we find that God's Spirit will always back our efforts. When we look for what God is doing in any given situation, His Spirit will give revelation, and His encouraging words and deeds will flow from within us.

I encourage you today to try and catch someone doing something right. Try to find one person to encourage with a kind word or generous deed. Give your time and resources to the least of those among you, and be reminded, that we are all the least of these. Look for the greater qualities in others and God will show you the greater qualities that He has placed within you. When you start to think, speak, and act like Jesus, others will see Him living in you and this will glorify our Father who is in Heaven.

Scripture References:

"So encourage each other and build each other up, just as you are already doing." (1 Thessalonians 5:11)

"Let no corrupting talk come out of your mouths, but only such as is good for building up, as fits the occasion, that is may give grace to those who hear." (Ephesians 4:29 ESV)

"Pleasant words are a honeycomb, sweet to the soul and healing to the bones." (Proverbs 16:24 NIV)

Think on Good Things

When we are new in the faith, God often reveals Himself in and through our pastors and mentors. It's such a great gift to have people in your life who are on the road ahead of you, who can lead you and guide you along the way like a spiritual GPS (God Positioning System). When we see Jesus clearly working in and through someone who the Lord has placed in our lives, it gives us great hope for our future, and also gives us confidence in the guidance we are receiving. When we know it is the Lord working and speaking through our mentors, even the correction that we receive will make us feel loved.

A great mentor can often trace problems back to their root cause. Many of my problems, especially early on in my walk, could be traced back to my thought life. I think that is why

Reverend Fred often ends our conversations with these edifying words: "Jeff, think on good things." He sees that I spend way too much time thinking about all of the evil that I so often see in this world, and I forget that where sin abounds, God's grace does more abound (see Romans 5:20). Often, when I have found myself down and out, Reverend Fred has shown me the way out through a change in my thought life. God's wisdom is always proved right by her actions, because the moment that I begin to shift my thinking to the goodness of the Lord, and all that He is doing in my life, and the lives of those around me, my disposition changes, and I feel His joy rise up inside me.

Reverend Fred has taught me well how to think like God thinks. He has done this by assuring me that God has given me both the desire and ability to think as He does (see Philippians 2:13). Through the operation and cooperation of the Holy Spirit in me, I can and will think like God thinks. To put this into Rev's vernacular, I can and will "think on good things" and I can do it with passion and purpose. I can think about how much the Lord loves everyone, even our enemies, and that He died for them just as much as He died for me. When I begin to think about the size of my sin, and depression tries to creep in, I can think of the Son, who took the weight of my sin on His cross, and that burden is lifted. When I think of the magnitude of the world's sin, as it closes in on me, I shift my thoughts from the sin to the Son, and the Son's light dispels all darkness. When I think of what Jesus did for me and for the entire world, the tears begin to flow like living water. Enough tears to wash the feet of Jesus and the feet of anyone in need of His cleansing.

So, I encourage you today, my friend, to think on good things. Start each day with prayers of praise for the forgiveness of all your sin—past, present, and future. And not only for your sin, but the sin of the entire world. Think on all of the good Jesus has done in your life and continues to do today through His Holy Spirit in you. Think of the day when you will meet Him face to face, and you will see Him in all of His glory. A glory so bright that you will need a new glorified body to handle the light, and a new glorified mind to comprehend the beauty before you.

Scripture References:

"And now, dear brothers and sisters, one final thing. Fix your thoughts on what is true, and honorable, and right, and pure, and lovely, and admirable. Think about things that are excellent and worthy of praise. Keep putting into practice all you learned and received from me – everything you heard from me and saw me doing. Then the God of peace will be with you." (Philippians 4:8-9)

"He Himself is the sacrifice that atones for our sins—and not only our sins but the sins of all the world." (1 John 2:2)

"Let this mind be in you, which was also in Christ Jesus: who being in the form of God, thought it not robbery to be equal with God: but made Himself of no reputation, and took upon Him the form of a servant, and was made in the likeness of men: And being found in fashion as a man, He humbled Himself and became obedient unto death, even the death of the cross." (Philippians 2:5-8 KJV)

The Man in the Middle

Jesus, of His own free will, chose to be suspended on a cross, no longer touching earth and not yet ascended into Heaven. It is here that He shed His precious blood which fell upon the earth, cleansing us from all sin—past, present, and future. With His once-and-for-all-time sacrifice, Jesus offered both His humanity and deity so that we could be freed from the tyranny of sin and be reunited with our Father in Spirit. As He hung on that cross, He was perfectly balanced between two criminals, one who was repentant and therefore able to see Him as Savior and the other who cursed Him bitterly with his dying breath. He truly was God's middle man. Fully Holy and without sin, so as to satisfy the righteous requirements of the Father's law, and fully man for the benefit and relationship of anyone who would receive Him.

In my walk with the Lord, I often grow weary by my own constant introspection. When I focus on what I am doing, instead of what Jesus has done for me, and is now doing in me, I find that I can frustrate the grace of God. When trapped in this state, the Lord often uses Reverend Fred to help me find my way out. He is able to redirect my path by redirecting my gaze to the man in the middle. The man who, while on this earth, perfectly walked that narrow path between grace and faith. And when He walked His perfect walk, and talked His perfect talk, He did it not only *for* us, but *as* us. His perfect performance was made on our behalf, and what He accomplished is now credited to our account.

Yes, Reverend Fred has taught me well, to take my eyes off myself and to cast them back on the man in the middle, who is always balanced perfectly between our humanity and our newfound holiness that we share in Him. In looking to Jesus, we no longer feel the pressure of trying to perform, because through His finished work on the cross, He has released to us (and in us) the Holy Spirit, who can now lead us and guide us through our spiritual union with Him.

We, in effect, have now become the hands and feet, eyes and ears and heart of Jesus, and we can show this dying world our resurrected Savior who has so perfectly balanced Himself within us. Yes, the man in the middle is very familiar with our human frailty, so we no longer need to be afraid to take chances and make mistakes, but can instead rest fully assured that as He is also holy, so too are we by our spiritual union with Him.

If we walk in the Spirit, we can do what is pleasing to Him and fulfill His will for our lives. And when we find ourselves bummed out by our flesh and down again, we have an advocate before the Father who reminds us that we are forever forgiven of our sin because the blood of Jesus has cleansed us from all unrighteousness.

As you work out your salvation today with reverential fear and trembling at the goodness of God, thank Him for the man in the middle. Thank God we have an advocate who is seated at the right hand of the Father. A middle man who intercedes for us in prayer. A middle man who faced every temptation that we face today so that He could relate to us, and to show us His way to new life through His resurrection.

Scripture References:

"For God's will was for us to be made holy by the sacrifice of the body of Jesus Christ, once for all time. Under the old covenant, the priest stands and ministers before the altar day after day, offering the same sacrifices again and again, which can never take away sins. But our High Priest offered Himself to God as a single sacrifice for sins, good for all time. Then He sat down in the place of honor at God's right hand. There He waits until His enemies are humbled and made a footstool under His feet. For

by that one offering He forever made perfect those who are being made holy." (Hebrews 10:10-14)

"For God is working in you, giving you the desire and the power to do what pleases Him." (Philippians 2:13)

"Looking unto Jesus the author and finisher of our faith; who for the joy that was set before Him endured the cross, despising the shame, and is set down at the right hand of the throne of God. For consider Him that endured such contradiction of sinners against himself, lest ye be wearied and faint in your minds. Ye have not yet resisted unto blood, striving against sin." (Hebrews 12:2-4 KJV)

Don't Give Up, Just Tighten Up

You might as well face it, at certain times in your life you are going to be a big disappointment to yourself. You are going to have moments where you let others down, where you let yourself down, and when you even feel that you have let God down. Jesus told us very clearly that in this world we would have trouble, and surely the hardest trouble to overcome is the trouble that comes from our own making. Even as a born-again, Spirit-filled believer you are going to do things that will surprise and shock you to your core. But take heart, you are no surprise to Jesus, who at one time took on your fleshly nature, and was Himself tempted in every way, yet thankfully was without sin. He knows all about human nature (your old dead nature) and He came to do something about it.

I have been so blessed to have a mentor like Reverend Fred, someone who I can go to when I am down so low that I don't even feel like getting out of bed. Many times, in my walk with the Lord, I have done things that have grieved me to my core. Without fail, Rev has always told me "Not to give up, but to tighten up." He has never condoned my sin, and yet has never made me feel condemned. It takes a very special person, someone who walks very closely with the Lord, to assure you that you are always forgiven in Christ. Someone who further assures you that through Christ you have been given strength in your spirit, and even the desire and ability to "Go and sin no more."

So many people get tired of themselves and tired of feeling that they have let everyone (including God) down, and often times simply give up in their walk with the Lord. I have learned from Reverend Fred over the years (after countless failures) that the best response to my greatest failure, should always be to press into the

Lord instead of walking away from Him. In doing so, I have found that He has truly provided unlimited forgiveness, and that He will forever pick me back up, dust me off, and assure me that my sins are forgiven through His shed blood. And as He sets me back on His path, with my tears of joy flowing, He assures me that I have the ability to "go and sin no more."

I have found and experienced firsthand that it is truly the kindness of the Lord that leads people to repentance (see Romans 4:2). It's that full assurance that He will never leave us and never forsake us, simply because His grace and mercy are inexhaustible. So, if and when you feel like a failure, just remember, "Don't give up, just tighten up." Don't run from the Lord when you blow it again, just run to Him. The more you do this, and the more He forgives you time and time again, the more you will fall deeper in love with Him, and before you know it, that habit or stronghold that kept you in bondage for so long, will be a thing of the past.

Press in and press on into the Lord Jesus, and the heavy packs and chains will fall off your body, and your spirit will begin to soar, and you will know and believe that God's love for you is something that you can never exhaust or exaggerate. You are forever forgiven, and that's what makes you forever free.

Scripture References:

"These things I have spoken unto you, that in me ye might have peace. In the world ye shall have tribulation: but be of good cheer, I have overcome the world." (John 16:33 KJV)

"They kept demanding an answer, so He stood up again and said 'All right, but let the one who has never sinned throw the first stone!' Then He stooped down again and wrote in the dust. When the accusers heard this, they slipped away one by one, beginning with the oldest, until only Jesus was left in the middle of the crowd with the woman, 'Where are your accusers? Didn't even one of them condemn

you?' 'No Lord,' she said. And Jesus said, 'Neither do I. Go and sin no more.'" (John 8:7-11)

"For this very reason, make every effort to supplement your faith with virtue, and virtue with knowledge, and knowledge with self-control, and self-control with steadfastness, and steadfastness with godliness, and godliness with brotherly affection, and brotherly affection with love. For if these qualities are yours and are increasing, they keep you from being ineffective or unfruitful of our Lord Jesus Christ. For whoever lacks these qualities is so near-sighted that he is blind, having forgotten that he was cleansed from his former sins." (2 Peter 1:5-9 ESV)

Every Day is Sunday with Reverend Fred

Did you know that under the Old Covenant the Sabbath Day begins at sundown on Friday and ends at sundown on Saturday? Under the New Covenant, the Sabbath is actually a place of rest where we abide 24/7/365 in the presence of Christ through our spiritual union with Him. I don't want to burst your bubble if you are part of the Sunday-nod-to-God crowd, and I want to strongly encourage you to continue to go to church on the day you enjoy it most, but please go only because you want to go.

One of the greatest lessons that Reverend Fred has taught me over the years is that church is not a place we go, but church is actually who we are. Under the New Covenant that Christ established through His finished work, the church has become the body of believers who have chosen, of their own free will, to walk in constant fellowship with Him through our shared union in the Holy Spirit. We are Christ's body, and wherever we go, God's mobile church goes to reach the lost, broken, and hurting. So, whether you are headed to the grocery store, or to a friend's house, or on a mission trip, you bring the new church of God where it is needed most. And it's needed most wherever you go.

Some of my most memorable encounters with the Lord have occurred while I was rolling with Reverend Fred, and many of them happened to us when we were on our way to somewhere else. Whenever the Lord sends us out (especially two by two), we can always go with great excitement and expectancy as we wait to see who He has placed in our path. I am reminded that when we minister this way, we are ministering the same way that Jesus did during His brief three-and-a-half-year ministry. Many of the people that He touched, healed, and inspired were ministered to while He was on His way to somewhere else—and for us today that pattern continues.

Whenever we encounter someone that doesn't know the Lord, our first reaction is often to get them to attend a Sunday service at our local church. And while there is nothing wrong with inviting someone to church, we should really shift our focus on bringing the church to them. When Jesus was around others, He always identified their greatest physical needs before He ever attempted to feed them with spiritual food. He was a need-meeter extraordinaire. He used His power to perform miracles like a dinner bell calling people to salvation. Calling people to a wedding supper that did so much more than just meet physical needs. Today, as believers, we possess the same Holy Spirit and therefore have the mind of Christ, and can do ministry/church in the very same way that He did.

I have been blessed to have a great mentor these past twelve years who has shown me what church should look like, a person who does church the way Jesus did church. And although my friend Reverend Fred does it imperfectly, he shows me that we have a perfect Lord working with us in all our weakness, to show Himself alive and faithful to those in great need. I encourage you by the grace of God, don't just attend church for one hour a week, but be the church 24/7/365. As you go, rest assured, Jesus is walking with you through the Holy Spirit.

Scripture References:

"There remains, then, a Sabbath-rest for the people of God; for anyone who enters God's rest, also rests from his own work, just as God did from His. Let us therefore, make every effort to enter that rest, so that no one will fall by following their example of disobedience." (Hebrews 4:9-11 NIV)

"Do you know that you are God's temple and that God's Spirit dwells in you?" (1 Corinthians 3:16 ESV)

"So then you are no longer strangers and aliens, but you are fellow citizens with the saints and members of the household of God, built on the foundation of the apostles and prophets, Christ Jesus Himself being the cornerstone, in whom the whole structure, being joined together, grows in a holy temple in The Lord. In Him you are also being built together into a dwelling place for God by the Spirit." (Ephesians 2:19-22 ESV)

Seeing Jesus in the Mirror

Reverend Fred always tells me that we can see Jesus everywhere if we are looking for Him. The Bible shows us very clearly that we can see Him in all creation, people, and circumstances by simply choosing to look for Him. What you seek, you will always find. So seek Jesus, and you will see Him all around you.

One day while sharing this truth with Rev, he informed me that there was one more place I needed to look for Jesus. He told me that I needed to start seeing Him in my mirror (see Colossians 1:27). He reminded me that my Bible is like a spiritual mirror, and that when I start to see who I am in Christ, and what I can do through Him, that the world around me will begin to change. That when we move in faith, the Lord's power is always present to move with us, thereby showing the world that Jesus is alive and well, and that He lives Spirit to spirit with us believers. He lives and moves today through His brothers and sisters, which brings glory to the Father of us all.

The scriptures remind us that God is Spirit, and that all He ever wanted was for us to be united with Him in Spirit, to be His spiritual offspring. God was made flesh in Jesus in order to pave the way for this perfect spiritual union. Jesus opened Heaven's door for us by living a perfect, sinless life under the law (Old Covenant) and then offering His body as God's final sacrifice for sin. His shed blood cleansed our spirits once and for all from ***all*** sin, allowing God to unite us with Himself eternally (see 1 Corinthians 6:17). Today the Holy Spirit reminds us moment by moment of who we are in Christ and He so willingly provides His power for us to walk as Jesus walked. The Lord Himself promised us that we would not only be able to do exactly as He did, but that we would be able to do even more! (See John 14:12.)

If you study the scriptures you will see that Jesus lives today in believers. We are the Lord's temple, and it is God's will for us to show this lost and dying world that Jesus is alive and well, and that His resurrection life and power is present in earthen vessels (see 2 Corinthians 4:7). Yes, if we are to see Jesus today and actually have an impact on this world, we absolutely must believe that we can see Him in our spiritual mirror. His presence and power is working through every believer, giving us the desire and the ability to do what pleases Him. And faith in Him is what pleases Him most!

It pleases Him when we receive the free gift of the Holy Spirit by faith, and boldly step out to do what He calls us to do. We need to stop waiting for God to move! It's our time to rise from our thirty-eight-year rest at the edge of the pool of Bethesda, and simply do what He says we can do in the exact way He says we can do it! If we are to see Jesus today, we need to start by seeing Him in the mirror. Look in the mirror and tell me friend, who's image do you bear?

Scripture References:

"And we, who with unveiled faces all reflect the Lord's glory, are being transformed into His likeness with ever-increasing glory, which comes from the Lord, who is the Spirit." (2 Corinthians 3:18 NIV)

"For if you listen to the word and don't obey, it is like glancing at your face in a mirror. You see yourself, walk away, and forget what you look like. But if you look carefully into the perfect law that sets you free, and if you do what it says and don't forget what you heard, then God will bless you for doing it." (James 1:23-25)

"For in Him we live and move and have our being. As some of your own poets have said, 'we are His offspring.'" (Acts 17:28 NIV)

"For God is working in you, giving you the desire and the power to do what pleases Him." (Philippians 2:13)

Walking Mark Home

I recently paid my first visit to Florida's death row with my mentor and best friend Reverend Fred. He has been making regular visits there for the past two decades, and many of the 360-plus men awaiting execution have come to know him both through personal experience and word of mouth. As we entered the bowels of what many consider to be hell on earth, my anxiety level rose with every iron door that slammed shut behind me. My breathing became labored as I realized how hopeless this place was and how helpless I felt in trying to combat this spirit of despair that was trying to overtake me.

As the final set of ironclad doors slammed shut behind us, and we walked down the first row towards the first cell, I was reminded by my mentor to keep my mouth shut (no problem because I was about to puke anyway) and to simply observe. "Hey there," he said to the first man who was lying on his cot with his lights turned off. The man arose and flipped his light on and began to converse with Reverend Fred. This man actually remembered him from a visit that he had paid him years ago, and the two began to reminisce and to laugh. That's right—to laugh! As they spoke, the Spirit of the Lord became very evident to me through the laughter that these two men were sharing. A laughter that caused the lights in the neighboring cells to come on one by one.

Prison is a place where laughter is rarely heard, but on that day, it rose through that cell block like a fresh cool breeze. One by one those men stood waiting for us as we moved down death row one cell at a time. It was a powerful and profound day I will never forget. My experience from that day has me thinking about Mark Asay, a man who spent most of his adult life on Florida's death row. After exhausting all appeals in 2017, Mark's three decade wait on death row had finally come to an end, and final preparations were being made for his inevitable execution. As part of the state's preparation process, any inmate scheduled for execution is allowed to select a pastor that he can meet with once a week during the final months leading up to his execution. It was no surprise to me when Mark selected my pastor, Reverend Fred, to walk him to his death.

I remember the day Reverend Fred called me to tell me about this new and unique assignment, an assignment we both agreed was both divine and unprecedented. During the final few months of Mark's life on earth, he and Rev were given the privilege of meeting for an hour or two at a time; to exchange words and expressions through the six-inch plexiglass that separated them. The exchange that took place between these two men will forever remind me of the grace of God that surpasses natural understanding.

In 1988 Mark was convicted and sentenced to death for the double homicide of both Robert

Booker and Robert McDowell, two men of color, in what the state of Florida alleged was a hate crime. This would be the first case in Florida's history where a white man was sentenced to death for killing a black man. And yet, when this alleged racist hater was asked whom he wanted to walk with him through his final days on earth, he selected Reverend Fred. I believe when someone truly sees the Spirit of Christ in another person, the color of the container is the last thing on their mind (see 2 Corinthians 4:7). I believe it's why you won't find one physical description of Jesus in the New Testament, and the only one you can find in the Old Testament (see Isaiah 53:2) reveals that Jesus was not physically attractive at all, quite the opposite.

Reverend Fred told me that during their very first visit, with only a few words exchanged, he knew by the Spirit of God that Mark was a born-again believer in our Lord Jesus Christ. Over the next several weeks it became very clear to Rev that this guy, whoever he may have been before, was a man who had been reborn by the Spirit of God. To quote Reverend Fred directly, "he didn't have a racist bone in his body." What better way to spend your final days on earth, or any time on earth for that matter, than to fellowship with a brother in Christ through the same Spirit. Yes, the one who removed blindness from so many, graciously allows our color blindness to remain.

During one of their visits, Mark explained to Rev how he had received the two racist tattoos which he still shamefully bore on his body. These two tattoos were instrumental in the state's allegation that Mark's crime was a "hate crime" (aren't all crimes hate crimes?). While serving time in a Texas prison at age nineteen, a very frightened Mark had sought protection by joining a group of racist haters who were more than willing to brand him. One tattoo on his elbow he would forever keep covered with a bandage, and the second one barely still visible he had attempted to burn off of his body in regret. Mark admitted to Rev that he had been drunk that night in 1988, furious from a drug deal gone wrong the night before, but race was never his motive. You can believe what you will, but only God knows our hearts this well, and only God has provided Jesus to change them through His spiritual rebirth.

Mark Asay was pronounced dead on August 24, 2017, at 6:22 p.m. from an experimental lethal injection administered by the state of Florida. With hundreds of protestors and news crews making quite a ruckus outside the walls of Florida State Prison, Mark breathed his final breath on earth, and we believe he was ushered into the presence of our Lord. In Matthew 6:22 Jesus says that when your eyes are completely focused on Him, that your whole body becomes full of light. I believe that Mark, at precisely 6:22 p.m., experienced for Himself the full light of God's presence in Christ. The colors he sees now in Heaven are not black and white, they are beautiful beyond our imagining and illuminated by the glory of the Lord Jesus Christ. May we all become color blind here in this life, and may we all long to see the colorful lights of Heaven revealed by the Glory of Jesus.

Interesting footnote: Since Mark's death in 2017, the Florida Supreme Court has issued a mea culpa *of sorts by acknowledging that one of Mark's victims, Robert McDowell (who was dressed in drag when Mark shot him) was actually not African American as the state had alleged, but was in fact from parents who were white and Hispanic.*

Scriptural References:

"My servant grew up in the Lord's presence like a tender green shoot, like a root in dry ground. There was nothing beautiful or majestic about His appearance, nothing to attract us to Him." (Isaiah 53:2)

"Some of us are Jews, some are Gentiles, some are slaves, and some are free. But we have ALL been baptized one body by one Spirit, and we all share the same Spirit." (1 Corinthians 12:13)

"But the Lord said to Samuel, 'Do not consider his appearance or his height, for I have rejected him. The Lord does not look at the things people look at.

People look at the outward appearance, but the Lord looks at the heart.'" (1 Samuel 16:7 NIV)

"After this I looked, and there before me was a great multitude that no one could count, from every nation, tribe, people, and language, standing before the throne and before the Lamb. They were wearing white robes and were holding palm branches in their hands. And they cried out in a loud voice: 'Salvation belongs to our God, who sits on the throne, and to the Lamb.'" (Revelation 7:9-10 NIV)

Conclusion

RUNNING WITHOUT LEGS

At the end of his often long days of ministry, Reverend Fred always looks forward to an egg sandwich that his wife Anita makes for him. Suffice it to say, there has been an occasion or two where he has told me, "I don't think there will be any egg sandwich tonight." And this because Rev had done something to rub Anita the wrong way. Yes, behind every good man, there is a woman rolling her eyes. Anita is the silent partner in a very blessed partnership forged together by the Lord Himself. She is the silent strength behind this great man of God, she is the tether to his balloon. She grounds him, prays for him, and encourages him day by day. Without Anita, there would be no Reverend Fred.

Neither Reverend Fred nor Anita know that I am writing this little book that you hold in your hands. If you're reading it in finished form, then by grace they have allowed me to share their story with you. A story about a less than perfect man, whom the Lord has used to shape countless lives in our little corner of the world and beyond. I hope that you have been inspired to see how one man, under the direction of the Holy Spirit, can show Jesus to a world that desperately needs Him. His life is proof that we can change the world one simple encounter at a time, by simple obedience to the Lord's command to "Go." And when we go, we must believe that the Holy Spirit will bear witness to the truth of the life of Christ in us, and for the sole benefit of those who need Jesus the most.

On our way out to Florida State Prison the other night, my friend Jim asked Reverend Fred, "Don't you think it's interesting how the Lord brought you and Jeff together? I mean you guys couldn't be more black and white, more from opposite sides of the track. Don't you think it's strange?" Reverend Fred paused, smiled, and simply replied, "Jim, I think it's divine." Some things are unmistakably from God.

Reverend Fred and I have spent most of our time together visiting inmates at Florida State prison. I seldom think about or mention the impact that he has made in our community through his frequent visits to local nursing homes. Early on in our relationship, I tried my hand at nursing home ministry, and let's just say it wasn't my cup of tea. Although we had several strange and wonderful encounters during my few nursing home visits, there was one visit that I will never forget.

Although I don't recall his name, I can still picture his long hair and his well-worn face which bore a smile as we entered his room. As we approached him lying in his bed, he began to shake his head back and forth and then exclaimed, "I can't believe you guys are here!" As we moved closer towards his bedside, and he pulled back his sheets, we could see that he that he was missing both legs. He then pointed to his wheelchair next to his bed and shouted, "Quickly, help me get into my wheelchair!"

Within a flash we had this man firmly seated in his wheelchair, and he immediately raced over to his dresser against the wall. He quickly opened the top drawer and began rummaging through his clothing, only to unearth his well-worn Bible. He then blurted out ten words that I will never forget, "I have been running from God for a long time." This prodigal son with no legs, could run no more.

As we lifted him back into his bed, with Bible in hand, he shared with us some of the many disappointments this fallen world had handed him. He shared about how he at one time was in good fellowship with the Lord, but like so many of us, wandered off and got lost along the way. It was my pleasure and privilege to watch my mentor and friend, Reverend Fred, lead this man back into fellowship with the Lord who had been waiting for him to come back home. With front porch lights brightly leading the way, this man walked right back into his Father's house. As we sat in that room reading our Bibles together, I was so full of joy, I felt so honored to be part of this divine encounter.

Perhaps today you find yourself tired out, weary, and worn out from this fallen world. Perhaps you have known the Lord, and have been known by Him, but have also strayed off the path. Perhaps you have never known the Lord at all, but are ready to make Him both Lord and Savior of your life today. If either of these scenarios describe you, I encourage you, in your own words, to ask the Lord Jesus into your heart, or to welcome Him back into your life. One thing I know for sure, He stands at the door of your heart and knocks. Just open up and let Him in.

About Reverend Fred

Reverend Fred Young is the team leader of MIND for Jesus Church in Jacksonville, Florida. This church without walls reaches inmates in ten local prisons through personal visits, preaching, teaching, and discipleship training. In addition to their robust prison ministry, Reverend Fred and his team also minister to the homeless, those in area nursing homes, and those living on the streets of Jacksonville. He is also a Volunteer Chaplain for the Florida Department of Juvenile Justice as well as a Volunteer Chaplain at Park Ridge Nursing home. Reverend Fred and his wife, Anita, have three adult daughters, Angela, Eunice, and Vanessa.

You may contact Reverend Fred at:

web: www.mindforjesus.com

Email: mindforjesus@yahoo.com

Address: P.O. Box 52622, Jacksonville, FL 32201

Fred & Anita Young

About the Author

Jeff Johnson is a passionate follower of Jesus Christ who loves to share his enthusiasm for God's Holy Word. As a Volunteer Chaplain at Florida State Prison, Jeff's ministry has a special emphasis on the wonderful benefits that believers can experience through the discipline of daily devotional time with the Lord. By trade, Jeff is Director of Sales for a generic drug manufacturer based in Mumbai, India. He and his wife, Kathleen, and their daughter, Kendall, live in Ponte Vedra Beach, Florida.

You may email Jeff Johnson at
Gospills@aol.com

Other books by Jeff Johnson:

Gospills Volumes 1, 2, and 3 –
See our five star ratings on Amazon.

Fred & Jeff

If you have enjoyed this book, please consider buying a copy for a friend and/or blessing us with a 5 star review on Amazon.